Big
Machines
At Work

Bulldozers

By Jean Eick

SCHOLASTIC INC.

New York Toronto London Auckland Sydney
Mexico City New Delhi Hong Kong Buenos Aires

For information regarding permission, write to:
The Child's World®, Inc.
P.O. Box 326
Chanhassen, Minnesota 55317

Photos: © 1998 David M. Budd Photography; p. 11 © Jack Fields/Corbis

ISBN 0-439-65054-2

Printed in the U.S.A.
First Scholastic printing, February 2004

Contents

On the Job

On the job, the bulldozer is a mighty machine. Instead of wheels, it has big **crawler tracks.** These big metal belts spin forward or backward to make the bulldozer move.

The bulldozer also has a huge **blade**

that crashes and bangs as it works.

The blade is a big, flat piece of metal that is very strong.

A bulldozer's blade can push over trees, and its crawler tracks can crawl right over fallen trees!

11

The blade can do other jobs, too. It can flatten big piles of gravel to make a new road.

Bulldozers are powerful enough to climb very steep hills.

The **ripper** on the back of a bulldozer is used to loosen rocks and concrete.

Then the blade can move them out
of the way.

Bulldozers move very slowly. They are loaded onto big trucks and moved from job to job.

19

Climb Aboard!

Would you like to see inside the **cab?** Climb aboard! The bulldozer's driver is called the **operator.** The operator's cab sits up over the big crawler tracks. It has all the controls that make the bulldozer work. The operator uses pedals, levers, and sticks to move the bulldozer and its blade.

Up Close

1. The cab

2. The crawler tracks

3. The blade

4. The engine

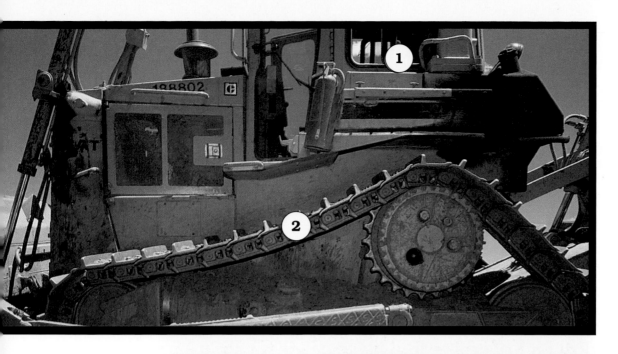

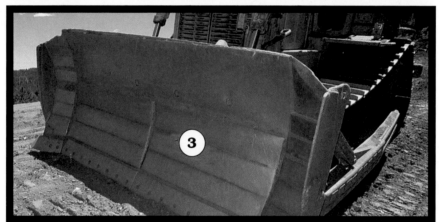

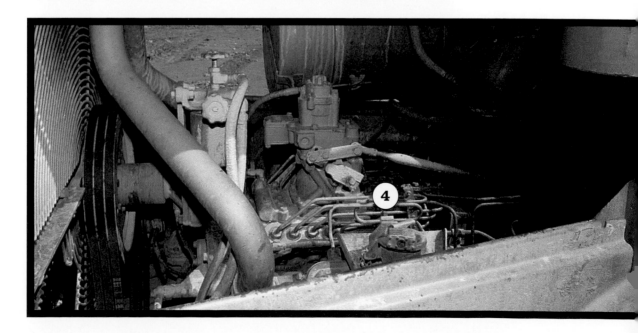

Glossary

blade (BLAYD)
A bulldozer's blade is a big, flat piece of metal that can push, scrape, and dig.

cab (KAB)
A bulldozer's driver sits in a place called a cab. It has a seat and the pedals, levers, and sticks that operate the bulldozer.

crawler tracks (KRAWL-er TRAX)
Crawler tracks are big metal belts that spin around to make the bulldozer move. They can spin forward or backward.

operator (OPP-er-ay-ter)
The operator is the person who drives the bulldozer and makes it work.

ripper (RIP-per)
The ripper is a strong metal arm on the back of a bulldozer. It moves up and down to loosen rocks and concrete so that the bulldozer can move them more easily.